THE
3 EVENTS!
FAITH, LOVE AND GOD

FRANK A. ISEDE

Contents

Thank you for purchasing this book, as it is the first book I have written. As a young boy, I never thought I would ever write a book someday, but here I am.

I know you might have many questions for me, as the title of this book might have stirred up curiosity. I didn't have a title when I started, and I prayed for vivid memories of events, as I write from the spirit and ask for guidance for clear transposition.

Here, I intend to share my experience and my truth, relaying my story for anyone out there who might find themselves in the same position or is just curious about their faith or God.

I will try to be detailed, and I have made efforts to break this book into chapters that flow from beginning to the end.

The Beginning

I grew up in a family of five. My father and mother didn't come from wealth. My dad was a security man who believed in doing everything right and treating fellow humans with the utmost respect. He made sure that we had respect for our elders by greeting them first and taught us to be humble.

I grew up in a Christian family. My father took us to church every Sunday, despite some Sundays as a young boy when I didn't feel like going. But he would rally everyone, and making it clear we had no choice but to go to church. Sundays were a must if you lived in our household.

We had what we called church clothes, which we only wore on Sundays. We dressed our best, and sometimes the same items were worn over several Sundays because my parents couldn't afford more church clothes. I often looked forward to Sundays because I looked my best on that one day of the week. A traditional Christmas gift from my parents was church clothes, which I always appreciated.

I grew up in a Pentecostal church, where I received all my teachings of the Bible from childhood. Much of it didn't mean a lot then, but enough exposure to the word of God certainly made sense later on in life.

In high school, going to church as a child felt like something that I had to do and sometimes felt forced, because my parents were strict on that point, doing what they thought was their responsibility as parents. I look back at those Sundays now and ask myself, *What if I hadn't ever stepped foot in church?*

But God never makes mistakes. I was set where I was in life by His hand.

If anything, going to church and learning about God exposed me to the power of something bigger, and I believed there was, but deep down, in my youth, I never experienced God. Or, at least, not as I would have liked. I knew that God was the supreme power that no one saw but was everywhere.

As I grew through high school, I went to a catholic school and was exposed to all kinds of Christian routines, the Catholic way; the hymns and the solemn, quiet prayers. This was indeed different from the Pentecostal way, how I was used to doing things. To elaborate, in the Pentecost church, I didn't have to confess my sins to anyone, I didn't have to go to church and expect a service or sermon called "Mass."

In high school, I began to develop curiosity as to why there were so many denominations and if God was the constant in all religion, as I had come to understand. If so, then why the difference in doctrine? I didn't think too much of it back in high school, as I was too busy with life, but I went to all the revivals, fellowships, and Bible classes when I could.

After high school graduation, and going through my first heartbreak, I began my first job. Soon, the reality of life started setting in. You know, the one you're going through right now. I noticed my parents started to let the pedal off the gas of going to church as a rule in our household, and I would skip some Sundays. After high school, my parents would often challenge me to get baptized, as I am old enough to make such decisions, but I stalled, until I realized it was something I must do to grow in my Christian life. At least, that's what I thought.

I went through the baptismal class at my Pentecostal church back in my early twenties. The class back then was to teach people like me the importance and significance of baptism.

Event One
Faith

After baptism, it felt like I was only checking a box. I didn't really feel any divine understanding of what I was doing. I just felt like it was something I had to do to fulfill the Christian part of my life.

I was still dedicated to understanding my religion, so I continued to go to church, and after a few years went by, I was able to secure a student visa to come to the United States.

It was a very anxious but exciting time of my life, as this was the dream of everyone I knew in Nigeria. Right before I left for the United States, my mother who was incredibly anxious about my trip, took me to her church, with a prophetic and gifted pastor. My first visit, I was told that I have a strong heart and my mother loves me. I wasn't shocked about that but rather was waiting for something more extraordinary from this man. I wanted him to tell me about my future or offer real guidance, but I got nothing. I later received a message from him that I needed to pray and fast for seven days. He instructed that I couldn't go home, and as part of their religion was to wear a white shirt and nothing colored.

I had to be in the church and just drink water at six p.m. This was called a dry fasting. I was hesitant at first, but I still proceeded to start the process. There were no cell phones, no TV, no books. Just one spirit with God. I wasn't sure what to expect going in.

Day one was all about reading verses from psalms and praying till I had no more words to continue. Then I'd sleep on the side of the church altar. Day two was a continuation of day one, all the way to day seven.

Through it all, from day one to day six, I had no experience of any sort. I was still praying to understand God and my relationship with Him, to feel something beyond hunger, but alas, I was left in silence.

I took part in each event at the church that week because I was living there at the alter for seven days. I was in their Wednesday Bible study, and everyone would leave and go home, while I remained behind.

On day seven, the final day before I had to break the seven-day fasting and prayer, I fell into a deep trance amidst worshipping God and calling God' names. I spoke His names, such as Jehovah Jireh, Jehová nessi, omnisciente, omnipotente God, and so forth, which carried on until I was half falling asleep, and all of a sudden, I heard a loud sound in my right ear. It sounded like a trumpet and a poking sound in my eardrum. I opened my eyes lightly and looked around to find out where the sound was coming from, but I was by myself there at the alter, with my Bible under my head as a pillow. When I didn't notice anything or see anyone, I fell back into the same trance. Then the sound came again, and this time a voice. The voice spoke fast. It sounded like multiple voices in synchronized, loud tone, saying "Deuteronomy six, verse one, Deuteronomy six, verse one,

Deuteronomy six, verse one." It spoke rapidly, repeating the chapter and verse three times.

I went straight to that passage in the Bible. I knew someone was trying to get me to read it right away. When I opened to the verse, the voice stopped.

Deuteronomy 6, verse 1, reads, using the King James Version:

1 "Now these are the commandments, the statutes, and the judgments, which the Lord your God commanded to teach you, that ye might do them in the land whither ye go to possess it.

2 That thou mightest fear the Lord thy God, to keep all his statutes and his commandments, which I command thee, thou, and thy son, and thy son's son, all the days of thy life; and that thy days may be prolonged.

3 Hear therefore, O Israel, and observe to do it; that it may be well with thee, and that ye may increase mightily, as the Lord God of thy fathers hath promised thee, in the land that floweth with milk and honey.

4 Hear, O Israel: The Lord our God is one Lord:

5 And thou shalt love the Lord thy God with all thine heart, and with all thy soul, and with all thy might.

6 And these words, which I command thee this day, shall be in thine heart:

7 And thou shalt teach them diligently unto thy children, and shalt talk of them when thou sittest in thine house, and when thou walkest by the way, and when thou liest down, and when thou risest up.

8 And thou shalt bind them for a sign upon thine hand, and they shall be as frontlets between thine eyes.

9 And thou shalt write them upon the posts of thy house, and on thy gates.

I stopped reading at verse nine. I looked around and knew I just experienced God for the first time through God's angels to deliver my message as I traveled to the United States.

This was a defining moment, as I was in amazement, lying flat at the altar.

I knelt and thanked God for the message, and I was never the same again.

I got up, and my mother came soon after to accompany me home. I told her what happened, and she smiled. She knew her son had just encountered God.

I was in awe and speechless. I knew in my spirit that I had just experienced God in such a way that I could never imagine or express.

For the first time, I felt like I looked crazy to the world. Then my mother and I went to the prophetic pastor, who I later told what happened, and he also smiled and told me that I was God's child and to remember I was of God when I went to the United States.

I then went home.

I took public transportation to go home, and all that way, I was still in awe. I thought no one except my mother would know or understand what I just went through. It was and is still an incredibly surreal experience.

I know each and every one of us have experienced God through a tough time, through something that you can't explain. I know there are many stories out there like mine. But the experience stayed with me, as I knew in my heart that there is a God. I've always known that God exists and loves me, but I never felt God the way I did that night on the alter.

After several months, I successfully migrated to the United States and touched down in New York. I brought sand in my pocket from Nigeria, which I poured as I stepped into New York, just outside the airport. Now, you might be thinking how did I bring sand in my pocket from Nigeria with all the immigration scanners. It wasn't much, just enough to sprinkle it and say a prayer of favor from God.

My destination was Louisiana, where I pursued my studies, attended fellowships, and continued my Christian journey.

I remember two incidents where God highly favored me and I knew God was with me. In my connecting flight from New York to Louisiana, the man who sat beside me sparked up a conversation and showed interest in my story, that I was flying to Louisiana alone, in a new country. He asked about where I would be staying, and I told him simply that I would pay for a hotel for three days, which cost about thirty-five dollars a night, till I could get in town and look for an apartment. I had $750 with me.

He was impressed with my fearlessness, and to my amazement, he was able to locate my hotel the next day, as it was a small town and I had told him its name. He had bought a bicycle and brought it to my hotel, giving it to me as a gift. He came with his wife and said, "This is America," and that I would need it.

I didn't understand then, but I do now. To go to the nearest Walmart or grocery store was an hour walk for me, and I was used to walking or catching public transportation in Nigeria. A small town in Louisiana was not Nigeria, and I soon came to appreciate that bicycle. I rode it everywhere, even on the highway. It felt weird that

I was the only one riding a bicycle everywhere, but I didn't think of it that much.

This was my first notable favor from God. It is quite interesting for me because now, as I sit down and remember all these events, I notice God has always been there. Every step of the way. It doesn't matter what you are going through or trying to figure it out. God is always there to make sure we have everything we need.

Life began to feel normal as I settled into my new life in the States. I found a church, where I would attend services and felt a sense of community. Then I moved with a new friend to North Carolina, where I began my pursuit of a better life, such as work and school. Then, suddenly, I got married.

It felt like a whirlwind love affair and marriage. I would seldomly attend church and then continue my fellowship with God. Often, I would attend house fellowship with my now ex mother-in-law, and through this small gathering, many questions would be answered for me about the understanding of the Word of God and the world.

I will never forget one instance when one of the brothers who fellowshipped with us asked the question, "Why do people judge us for the way we dress and for keeping the sabbath day holy? There are so many judgements and expectations." I remember, that night, we all looked at each other and couldn't reference the Bible at that point in time to answer that particular question, which puzzled us on what the Bible says about that. It's a hard reality we face in this world that we live in. Although the saying "don't judge a book by its cover" almost feels like a coverup, it's not far from the truth. We are all judged or at least quantified by something external.

That question sat in my mind, until next day, when, suddenly, at the same fellowship, the spirit led me to a verse that I had never come across before or heard in any preaching I had ever been to. The verse I read out loud opened my eyes, to the amazement of my fellow brothers and sisters. We all looked at each other and smiled, because we knew God was with us to answer that question, and I felt honored that I could be a vessel.

Colossian 2:16 reads: *"Let no man therefore judge you in meat, or in drink, or in respect of a holyday, or of the new moon, or of the sabbath days."* The verse went on to talk about how everything eventually perishes, and in chapter three, it starts with focusing your heart to the things above and not of this earth.

Indeed, this answered some of my own questions about following doctrine and cultures and religion. It was an incredible night and revelation. That night exposed that we all could have the same understanding of God if we asked and waited for guidance through the Word of God, the Bible.

God talks to us through any means, but one notable way is through the Bible, and that's why it became important to me to write this book. I have started to read my Bible almost every day.

After that night, I got a new job and started working, and my wife got pregnant with our first daughter. This changed my life, literally. I suddenly felt so much love for the little human we created. I opted to be a stay-at-home father and watched her grow for two years, until our divorce.

During this period of staying home, I began to feel depressed and tired of the marriage. It felt like a dark time. My wife and I were in a bad place in our relationship. I found myself far from God and was forgetting my message and the power of God.

Eventually, we filed for divorce, and I moved to Texas from North Carolina, where I started anew. It was one of the hardest decisions of my life, but I felt I had to do it for a better life and chasing my American dream.

We worked out custody, where I went to pick up my daughter during summer break. I began working at Lowes and started my life.

All this time, I would seldomly go to church and wasn't as devoted. Well, you could say I started to live life, and eventually, I stopped attending church and began figuring out life on my own.

Being on a fixed income working at Lowes, I managed my life and remained steadfast to my goals. Then someone hit my car in my apartment, an Acura 3.2TL. So, I needed another car. I went to buy a vehicle, and the finance manager who recognized my name as a Nigerian came out and talked with me to apply for a job and sell cars.

Up until that time, it never occurred to me to sell cars. I took the application and never applied. I found it odd that the finance manager took time to call me often and persuade me to apply to sell cars, and I remember him telling me that I shouldn't forget where I'm from when I 'start making good money,' as he put it. I still didn't apply.

Then, one day, on my day off, I decided to apply and went to four dealerships with brands like Toyota, Honda, Mazda, and a used car dealership. I went with my gut feeling, as I felt at home at the Honda dealership, where I was hired on the spot. I ended up talking with four different managers, who took an interest in me and my pitch on why they should hire me.

I was hired and sold twenty-six cars my first month, making in one month what I used to make in one year at Lowes. My single self went with friends to the club and had the best night of my life. Or so I thought, because with so much alcohol, I can't remember if it was the best night or it was just an illusion.

After four months of work in sales and being successful, I met my second wife. We had a one-night stand shortly after meeting for the first time, as it was a whirlwind of attraction. I still remember telling her that I had a child from a previous marriage after just having sex with her, and she was astonished how she didn't know me and we just had sex. That moment stuck with me because I learned something important about my current generation, that relationships often occur this way. There's a reason God saved sex for after marriage.

A few weeks later, she gave me the news most single guys are afraid to get. "I didn't get my period." She got pregnant just a few weeks after dating, and I was terrified because I never wanted to have a child out of wedlock, as I wasn't raised that way. This was coupled with the fact that I already had a child with my first wife and was raising the child outside of marriage. It felt like I was failing myself and failing God and my parents.

Up to this time, I seldomly attended church or built a relationship with God. It felt like I was on my own sometimes.

After much contemplating about how to address the issue of her pregnancy, we decided to move in together and get married, as I was strongly against having a child outside of wedlock. At some point, she was fine with raising the child on her own, but I insisted we get married. My parents were fine with me raising the child outside of wedlock, but I ignored all opinions.

I proceeded to marry her, and we moved in together. We had our first baby together and bought our first home.

I invited my mother to visit us in the United States. When my mother visited and met my new family, it was a great revelation, as I saw another side of my wife. I noticed a few characteristics of concern to me that if asked at that point and I knew before what I knew then, I wouldn't have married her. My answer would have been a no.

After eight years of a long marriage and losing my purpose and relationship with God, we were blessed with two beautiful children and a beautiful house in a nice suburb. I felt like I had it all, even though deep-down, happiness and tranquility were far from my heart.

We decided to end the marriage and file for divorce after too many lies and hurts. It was the healthy and right thing to do. I had ignored everything she told me about our compatibility. She would often tell me that she didn't feel like I was her person and our compatibility was off.

I learned something big in that fallout, and I felt lost for the first time.

Event Two
Love

The divorce took almost one year to finalize because of the back and forth for the division of property. We ended up foreclosing our home and losing a hundred thousand dollars in the down payment made to purchase the home one year prior.

It became vicious, both willing to lose everything as long as no one won. But in reality, the children lost more than we hoped.

It was a low point in my life, as I felt lost and clueless in my direction. I remember one evening sitting down and waiting for my lawyer to report back to me on our never-ending mediation to discuss terms. I was feeling down and alone and hopeless on that day because the divorce was sucking the life out of me. We lost so much to the divorce that I suffered financially, as I was the bread winner and she was a stay-at-home mother of our two children. It was a low point for me, because I had envisioned a perfect family and worked toward unity and prosperity.

At this point, I was empty, and I started to go to clubs or parties to fill the void. I dated and cheated on a few dates. I was looking for quick fixes to my problem of loneliness. I would book short trips to Dominican Republic and Thailand just to have a short-term fix of fun. When I returned home, I felt empty and lonely at night.

Now that I think about it. I didn't even stop for a second to go to church and find my way to God. I don't even know why.

After much anguish, my divorce became final after my last trip to Colombia for a quick fix of fun.

It was a dark time. I am not proud of those times, but living in the dark blinds you from yourself.

I have always had a desire for marriage and building a family, as it has always been my dream. Then, two weeks after my second divorce, I met a woman who lived in Colombia, though she was originally from San Cristobal, Venezuela, and we hit it off on Instagram.

We chatted every day and got to know each other more. Off course, this time, everything was on the table, and I had my boxes to check. We talked about personality, past, finances, religion, family background, and ideologies.

I started to develop feelings for her without really knowing her in person. I think what contributed to that was getting to know each other without mixing sex into it.

We chatted daily, morning and night for two months and learned about each other. I then booked a flight to Colombia to meet her in person. When I saw her at the airport, I knew within me that I would marry her. My heart felt at peace. Yes, I know what you might be thinking by now, as I often thought about it. I needed to take my time and find myself. I needed to focus on me while I sorted things out and get back on my feet. I've heard it all. But I realized that God's timing is not ours. We are on God's time, and God can do whatever He wants with us according to His time.

Up until this point, we'd briefly talked about our religions, as I told her I was a Christian and she told me she practiced Yoruba religion. I almost found it amusing because I was birthed in Yoruba land and knew the religion, as it had migrated from Africa to Latin America decades ago.

I didn't think too much of it, as I didn't know if I was going to end up with her long term, up until I met her in person.

We had a great time and got matching tattoos of our zodiac signs. It was a sign of something new starting. We then made a pact to be together forever. We also tattooed 'Forever' on our wedding ring fingers.

I couldn't believe I fell in love just two weeks after my divorce. I remember visiting her house for the first time and saw all the carved gods named orishas in the Yoruba religion. I wasn't afraid, because at that point, I was sure of my God and who I believed in. However, it became apparent that it was an issue I needed to resolve later.

After I returned from my trip to meet her, we continued our conversation and grew deeper in love with each other. Then, my issue with her religion started to become apparent, because she would often go to a river and perform some sacrifice, which was foreign to me as a Christian. Meanwhile, I hadn't found my way back to building my relationship with God, but I knew when something didn't look right spiritually.

I began to get angry at myself for falling in love with a woman from another religion. I asked why God would allow me to suffer again. Why did I fall in love with her so quickly? It was a daily battle that I wrestled with. We would often talk about how we could coexist with our Gods.

Then I told her as for me and my household, we would serve the lord.

Even though I wasn't really doing much serving the lord then, I had the conviction of my God and my savior Jesus Christ.

She would cry, and I would end the conversation, trying to build distance from her, though my heart was with her already.

I remember one night driving home from work and crying in my car, asking God, "Why, why, why? I have suffered too much and all I want is a woman who fears God, is respectful and gets along with my mother. It's not too much to ask. Why this woman with a different god? No. No. No!"

All of a sudden, I heard a voice like an imprint in my spirit, saying, "Your job is to love her."

I got this impression and felt that's what I would do. That night, I called her and said, "I will love you and show you love no matter what god you serve but on one condition. You can't have your idols in our home but you can practice your religion, and we can have two religions at home." She appeared happy about my decision, and that night, she was physically happy and content with it. I told her I would go with her to see her dance to her gods and be there for her but not partake in anything, which was fine with her, and I could see the relief in her face.

At this point, I was beginning to understand that God had not abandoned me and was still with me, even though I felt lost. I began to pay attention to myself and focus on my goals in life.

Event Three

God

Our love grew deeper and stronger. I showed her love, and up until this point, I hadn't found my way to build relationship with God and going to church. I was ashamed to tell my parent about her religious believe, as I knew I would be criticized for making bad choices with women and my life for my future.

But we continued our relationship, and our love for each other blossomed. Then, suddenly, I started to notice my left foot was dirty or had a blueish dark mark on my left toenails. I would wash it up as I showered, and I continued to notice it regularly and would often hear noises in my sleep. Then it became apparent that I got these marks when I slept on my toenails on my left foot.

Then fear started to set in, and I told my mother what was going on and would wake up to show her the markings. She and I assumed dark magic and thought maybe my ex was trying to kill me using dark magic. I could hear my mother praying even louder and harder for me. I often tried to stay up all night to avoid the mysterious markings, but I would still get it even after passing out for a second. It felt like something in the spirit realm was watching me, I grew increasingly afraid to see the markings, and it became more consistent. I would get cold chills, and I still get cold chills and sweaty writing it now. I started to look for ways to avoid it, for example, I would work longer hours, wear socks, and eventually I read online to buy sage and mirrors. I bought white sage as advised online and opened my windows and prayed against all evil spirits. But that didn't stop the markings, and I became increasingly frustrated and scared and helpless.

My mother gave me her anointed olive oil, which I would rub and make the sign of the cross on my feet. That would help in the morning, but it would be replaced with voices in my head as a sensation that something or someone was standing right next to me. I lived alone, and I couldn't go sleep in hotels, as I knew this was spiritual more than anything.

I had to tell my wife, while we were still dating and going through life. She told me she would consult her gods and find out who needed my attention or who was doing that to me. I needed an answer from anyone. I just wanted to have sound sleep. I wanted it to stop!

I remember going to my church to buy the sign of the cross and bought three and built an altar in my bedroom, hoping if it was an evil spirit, they would run away. Well, I'm sorry to break it to you; I still got the markings, and I became restless. This time, I was going to church, and I started to renew my faith. I thought by doing this, maybe it would stop it.

Then, one Sunday, my wife, which at that point we were still dating, told me she consulted her gods, and they said I have an ancestor I need to pay attention to. I was puzzled even more, as which of my ancestors did I need to pay attention to? I knew from my understanding of God that we don't pay attention to the dead, so it must be someone the gods cannot say or were at liberty to say clearly.

That Sunday, I called a spiritual guide. I do not want to say psychic because it carries a negative reputation. I called her feeling helpless and down. She at once connected with me over the phone, and we had never met before.

She told me, "Oh, wow, you were a disciple of Jesus, and those markings are from you walking and doing God's work."

As soon as she finished those words, it was like something lit up in me, and I said yes. I do feel like I am. She told me she had never seen such reading before, and it was amazing to share with me. She told me I needed to go back to church fully and serve God. That I was not giving God attention and my services were needed.

I was not amazed or shocked. I knew something inside of me was off track on my path.

After the phone call, I fell on my kneels and cried and prayed to God for the first time after such a long time. I cried because I could not believe it took extreme measures for God to show me, "Son, I love you, and I have been with you all this time. Look at me, son. You don't have to suffer, as my son Jesus has paid it all. I want and need your relationship."

Oh my God, I cried like a baby, and the next Sunday, I showed up early to church to recommit. I had attended the same church randomly, and after ten years, I became a member and signed up to be a door greeter and usher.

Then, suddenly, the markings stopped, and the strange noises stopped, and I started to fall asleep as normal. I felt the protection of God. I felt God and an assigned angel with me. It was a divine feeling to know God was with me, I have an assigned angel, Jesus lives in me, and I have all the authority against anything.

The picture on the front of the book is my actual foot and the marking, as I would take pictures of it when I noticed it. This is one of the clear pictures I took of it.

I felt like a superhuman. I felt strong because we wrestled not against flesh and blood but against principalities and powers. We need to have the whole armor of God.

My wife was amazed to see my growth and revelation, though she was still steadfast with her religion. But now more than ever, I was more committed to my God—the one true God. It felt like the second calling after my first encounter in Nigeria before I moved to the United States and had this second encounter.

As I write this book, and up to this point, I still can't hold in my feelings and am crying right now again just remembering that God loves me and us so much.

God's love for us is deeper than we think. God is amazing and even went to the extreme of sending his son Jesus so we can have a full relationship with him. In the beginning, yes, Genesis 3:8 states that the LORD God was walking in the Garden of Eden in the "cool of the day," which implies a specific time, often interpreted as the evening or late afternoon, to interact with Adam and Eve. Before their sin, God had regular, familiar communion with the first humans, and this instance describes a specific visit for confrontation after the Fall. So, this passage showed me that God has always wanted a relationship with us. That's why we were created in his own image.

After this realization, I started a spiritual journey of revelation and understanding. I started to read my Bible daily and founded a meeting with a small group of Christian men on Wednesday mornings at six-thirty a.m. before work. I was growing in God's knowledge and leadership. I started to listen to God's voice as it imprinted in my spirit. That still small voice as a voice of reason. We all have it there, but the noise of life has made us tune it out. God is there and Matthew 7:7 clarifies this by saying *"Ask, and it will be given to you; seek, and you will find; knock, and it will be opened to you."* Meaning, if you only ask and seek. God is right there. Regarding prayer, the book of Matthew indicates where to pray. In your closet or inner room. God wants our relationship and God is jealous, too.

I started to experience spiritual things and do what the spirit says, for example, after a few weeks, the spirit told me to start tithing, and I have never given ten percent of my income ever as a Christian. I often thought that God was might and didn't need my ten percent. Yes, this is true, but God told me, "I don't need it, son, but if you can trust me and you say you love me, give me your ten percent and watch if I won't bless you." By this time, I had just gotten out of a divorce, and I was going through one of the worst financial crises I had ever gone through. I was in shock that God would put this in my spirit this early, and I really needed every penny to pay debts. I even told my wife, when we were dating, and we had different views about it.

One Sunday at church, the pastor preached about tithe, and there it was again. I learned quickly when God is talking to you to do something, just do it. You cannot run or hide. Just like a father teaching a child all ways and lessons of life. God will do it through everything you see around you, if only you look to see and listen to hear.

It was a powerful sermon, as the pastor was able to depict me exactly as I was. I remember he used a bucket or some sort to explain that you are so blessed, then you have it, but at the end, you don't have it to achieve what you need. Like a continuous circle, but God allowed us one time for us to test God through tithing. I was sitting there at church and smiling because I looked up and said, okay, okay, okay. I get it. I commit to tithe for the rest of my life on earth. I committed that Sunday, and my first income came. It was hard because I knew I could use that ten percent to meet the minimum payment due, but I had to because who was the ruler of heaven and earth, who could take my life right now, who gave me favor, who could order favors? God. God can.

I decided to tithe, and I can tell you it increased my love for God because I felt more connected to Him. Then my prayer changed the following week because I started to remind God in my prayers. God, you said you would bless me. You said in your Word to give You ten percent and watch You bless me. It was amazing that I started to have so much confidence, like I went to the gym and got six packs overnight. Well, I'm working on that. I still have a little one pack. Give me time!

It's amazing how when you trust God and have faith, then your prayers change. You start to pray bold prayers, and your love for God grows.

After couple of months, one evening. My wife and I were video calling as a routine, when she broke down and cried and really told me what she was feeling. All I did was listen to her. She explained she had gone through so much with her religion, and with what she was learning and seeing with me and my God, she no longer wanted to do it anymore. I was dumbfounded.

I said, "You are like a mother priest and have performed so many sacrifices in that religion." She was like a pastor in that religion, and she was looked up to. She went into so many dark secrets that I don't want to repeat, and seclusion, and she saw my heart and my ways, and she wanted to feel freedom like I felt. I got the cold chills again as I remembered that night I got the message in my spirit that my only job was to love her despite everything I saw. I went back to that night I cried, asking God why.

I learned something very important that night. The Bible is for love and not judgement. God is love and love is God. Just by loving her and loving her as God loves me unconditionally made the difference in the world, and God taught me a big lesson about judgement and my job here. It's all about love!

At this point, I was astonished, as my wife cried and decided that night to renounce that god and all she'd ever done for it. She told me she felt like she was in bondage and scared for her life, as they told her that she would die if she left, and so on.

Well, that didn't come without a backlash for me. That night as I was sleeping, I started to choke, it felt like someone was choking at me spiritually, and I couldn't breathe. I was able to get the words out, "The blood of JESUS," and I got some relief and was able to recite the word of God at that moment as I yelled from my sleep, rebuking that god my wife worshiped out of my mouth in my room. I yelled the name of that water goddess. I yelled it like I knew in my spirit that it was her from my deep sleep. I yelled that god's name and opened my eyes as I recited Ephesians 6:12 KJV: "*For we wrestle not against flesh and blood, but against principalities, against powers, against the rulers of the darkness of this world.*"

Then I said, the battle had been won, and I felt strong and victorious that night. I smiled because I felt the victory.

I couldn't wait to tell my wife that morning what happened, and I did. I had a significant revelation that night that there was a constant war going on in the spiritual realm, which is a battle of souls. It is going on as you are reading or listening to this book. I just hope she believed me, because sometimes sharing these kinds of things with someone who might not understand could lead you to the psycho ward. When I told her, she shrugged and was amazed that her god attacked me because she thought the god of water was a kind, sweet goddess. I told her the truth, and my victory, and told her she was mine now and I had won the fight. She was totally mine. She belonged to God, and she was a child of God.

I have never felt so strong in my life than that moment. I had this feeling like Johnny Bravo. It has been surreal, my spiritual journey thus far. It's been a series of events back-to-back.

After that night, I have slept like a baby knowing my God watches over me day and night, and I am in God's safe hands.

I love God so much, and I pray every day that God is seen through me and not me. As my wife was able to see God and turn, so I want to live the rest of my life in His grace. My wife gave her life to Jesus with me, I bought her first Bible, and she was grateful. She is now a born again Christian and reads her Bible almost every day. We are growing together with the purpose of God, and we both walk our paths in life. I have the most peace and tranquility. I know exactly where I am going. It is so reassuring to know that and live internally free and at peace. Amazing!

As I began to read the Bible almost daily and pray, I began to understand so much about our God. We often look for answers, and sometimes in the wrong places or from the wrong person. God started to expose me to test of faith and my spirituality. Yes, as a Christian, we are subjected to temptations allowed by God to see our growth. We all have challenges and addictions. I went through a test on forgiveness, as I often hold grudges. I defeated my own body toward a desire to watch porn. Things that are not right and your spirit tells you. The truth is that we all have the truth inside of us and know what to do. We often opt for quick fixes, which leads to the end of us. I felt strong that my own body or self-desires could be conquered.

In the book of Matthew and Luke, of the King James Version (KJV) Bible, Jesus fasted for forty days, then he was led into the wilderness by the Spirit to be tempted by the devil. The devil, of course, saw an opportunity to tempts Jesus three times, offering him physical bread, suggesting he prove his deity by leaping from the temple, and finally offering him all the kingdoms of the world if he would worship the devil. Jesus resisted each temptation by quoting Scripture.

He came as man to show us how to live, went through everything to show us how to resist temptation, and after he rose, now he lives in us so that the light shines through us.

I have given my life completely to God. The truth is found through Jesus, who is the only way to God. And the beginning of the fear of God is the moment you begin to grow in wisdom.

My story is about real events in my life and my accounts of events that got me to this point. We all have our own story and journey this far. One thing I know is that we have a path and everything comes together for God's purpose. Some might be a sign, a miracle, or something extraordinary. But one thing remains constant; God is the same yesterday today and forever more. The heaven and earth shall pass, but God is constant.

As a child of God, I am enjoying learning and growing in the Word of God, as we should if we really seek His kingdom, because even though we are here, we set our eyes to the things above.

You might be in a position where you have never felt like God even exists. This is a good position because curiosity is a starting point and looking in the right direction to quench that thirst.

God is here, and my life is a testament that God's love for us is overwhelming, and it is free. My case might have been extreme with the markings and nudging in the right direction, but what if you are looking in the wrong direction. While on my quest of understanding something bigger, I found out we are all in search of something. Either we are chasing career growth, finances, children, ourselves, marriage, spiritual growth, or whatever it might be. But the true answers lie within us and looking in the right direction. Now, who knows what the right direction is?

As I remember, Numbers 21:8, "*And the Lord said unto Moses, Make thee a fiery serpent, and set it upon a pole: and it shall come to pass, that every one that is bitten, when he looked upon it, shall live.⁹ And Moses made a serpent of brass, and put it upon a pole, and it came to pass, that if a serpent had bitten any man, when he beheld the serpent of brass, he lived*."

All along, it has been the cross, and now looking at the cross and accepting Jesus opens the door to God, who is right there with you, waiting for you to look.

As of the writing of this book, I am still growing in understanding of God, and my love for God is ever strong. My relationship with my wife is healthy and strong, as well as with my children.

I have come to appreciate life more and the short time I have on earth. Every day is a gift that I am happy to receive and rejoice in it. I don't preach the Word of God because my life has become the Word of God. Now, I understand that we are supposed to radiate God's love to attract other people to want to feel that love, and we simply point to the cross.

I want to touch on tithing. As soon as I started to pay my tithe, I want to report to you that as of the writing of this book, God gave me divine creative freedom to create a candle business named "The Lamb Candles." I often wonder why the spirit would lead me to making candles. We as children of God are a sweet-smelling savor to God through prayers, and I was able to use beeswax and fragrance to come up with a unique scent. There you have it—I started a business while still working full-time, and the spirit led me to write my first book. Something that I have never thought about doing.

I have begun to expect the goodness of God. It is amazing to walk and have a relationship with Him.

The three major events in my life came about when I looked back at my experience, and I have picked these three events as a defining moment in my life. Indeed, life is a lesson, but what are we learning? There are so many questions and no right answer. Though it might seem like that, the first calling for me signified faith, because if you want something from your father, you won't eat until you get it. It is different. Jesus fasted, and as Christian, there is something spiritual about fasting. Depriving yourself of food and necessity because you are building relationship with your father.

The second event was love. I had to feel the love of God on my life in the lowest point of my life, and God picked me up and give me someone I fell in love with. Someone I asked him for. I often ask, "God, I married twice and divorced. I have sinned." God reassured me that once you are a new creation, you are new and everything is absolutely forgiven.

God allowed me to go through certain things, but those things didn't consume me. God never lays too much to handle on us, but everything for a purpose. I learned everything is for a purpose and a season.

Self-condemnation and the struggle for perfection often keep us in bondage to ourself. I used to think I wasn't perfect because I am human. Well, as a sinful human, you can't be. Allowing God to be in control and accepting Jesus changes everything. I got to a passage where God revealed to me that we are perfect in Christ, and as we allow God to be in control of our lives, we put on the whole armor of God. We are ready to face anything. Matthew 5:48 is a verse that states, "*be ye therefore perfect, even as your Father which is in heaven, is perfect.*" Jesus in this verse challenges us as he was preaching on the Mount.

Do not feel condemned and unclean. God loves us too much to reject us at any point. God allowed me to go through divorce just to come to depend on God and see God. Everything and all things are for God's purpose.

The third event was the marking on my foot, which signified the last calling. This event revealed the extent to which God will go for your attention. I sit here burning a candle made with beeswax that I created from my spirit, reflecting on how God, time and time again, has gotten the attention of His children. Let go through them, Exodus Chapter 3. While tending his father-in-law's sheep, Moses encountered the Angel of the lord in a flame of fire from a bush that burned but was not consumed. God then called to Moses from the bush, identified Himself as the God of Abraham, Isaac, and Jacob, and commissioned Moses to lead the Israelites out of Egypt. The story of Balaam is found in the Book of Numbers 22. As a hired prophet who was supposed to curse the Israelites, Balaam is rebuked and redirected by God through the miraculous speech of his own donkey.

Is God trying to get your attention, but life is just too noisy these days? God is still the same yesterday, today, and forever, and there are so many stories of miracles every day of God's work.

My prayer every day now is to thank God for everything I have and what God is doing. To listen and be a servant to God's children. We all are from God, and we are to serve each other according to God's will.

I pray that your journey is for something bigger—for God's purpose.

God bless you.

I thank God for allowing me to write a book using God's name, and Jesus for dying for me and affording me this mercy. A portion of the proceeds will go to the expansion of the ministry of God.

The 3 Events! Faith, Love and God
© 2025 by Frank A. Isede

Published by Frank A. Isede
Magnolia, Texas, USA

ISBN: 979-8-9933278-2-2

Printed in the United States of America

Scripture quotations are from the the Holy Bible, unless otherwise indicated.

First Edition, 2025

www.ingramcontent.com/pod-product-compliance
Lightning Source LLC
Chambersburg PA
CBHW071354130626
46556CB00005B/2184